The Uranus Complex

The Anthology of Reflective Awareness and Growth

Shanikqua Renee Palmer, LCSW

Dedication

This collection of work is dedicated to my parents, husband and children, who continue to inspire me to express truths that matter.

Preface

After a long 10 year journey of soul searching and building self-awareness and confidence through lyricism, music and astrology; I decided to record my late night thoughts, experiences, truths, trials and growth in the form of poetry. Therapeutic and mind shifting, writing poetry has allowed me to become emotionally intelligent and express my uncomfortable truths and comfortable lies. In society, we become accustomed to flocking with birds and in turn, we lose our core identity while simultaneously becoming a yes-woman/man. And this is something I no longer wanted to do. Herewith, at the age of 27, I began to write as a coping mechanism. The process of writing poetry was not an easy task as it, in its essence, became shadow work. My very own unconscious and repressed aspects as well as traumas were resurfaced and it was quite difficult to manage these emotions while juggling the many hats of being a mother of three, a wife, a daughter, friend, and licensed social worker. But I dedicated my time to completing this collection of work for myself; because if I'm not well, my family isn't either.

Welcome to the **Uranus Complex**; a strong placement in my personal birth chart that has allowed me to express emotions associated with extremes, breakthroughs and breakdowns, limitlessness, outcast behaviors and revolutionary visions. I hope you enjoy my thoughts, and remember, "I'm an artist and I'm sensitive about my shit" (Erykah Badu).

Namaste

Acknowledgements

I would like to acknowledge the extraordinary debt I owe the people in my life who have supported and empathized with my developmental and spiritual growth over the past 10 years. I first and foremost would like to thank my grandmother, who is now in heaven with the most high. Ms. Patricia Ann Pearl Palmer was and still is my guiding light and roots for me every chance she gets. She often speaks through me and pushes me to limits I never believed I was capable of achieving.

I would also like to thank my parents, Hope and Chappy, for always providing empathy, grace, realistic advice, truth and safety. If it weren't for them; I don't know where I would be in life. Another shout out to my dad for always telling me to "watch my ass." It is the best advice you can provide someone as it is a reminder to be safe and always remain covered with blessings. Thank you to my God mother as well, Cheryl Renee. Thank you for being my first level of spiritual convenant and keeping my mom calm whenever I got in trouble (haha).

Next I would like to thank my husband who encourages me to get up every day and chase my dreams. At times my dreams can appear cloudy and a never ending target, but that never deters him from being one of my biggest cheerleaders. I also must show love to my children; Destyn, Sevyn and Phoenix. Without them, there would be no me and I would have never been afforded the opportunity to dig deep within myself to understand love and self-worth. My family gives me hope and resiliency and I love them so much.

Another acknowledgement goes to my mother-in-law, Shimika. We have had our ups and downs, but you have always kept your word and continued to remind me that you are a woman first and will always be there for us. A great level of appreciation to my grandmother-in-law, Mema. You introduced me to scholarly literature and assisted me in opening up the portal to racial identity, self-awareness and love.

Lastly, I want to thank all those who I have come in path with or those who I have closely worked with. I also want to give a big praise to many others who have been in the trenches with me and accept me for who I am. Shout outs to Anaiah, Lyvette, Akilah, Lia, Leah, Amani, Lashawn, David, Crystal, Nyree, Lola, Ester, Charisma, Shynequa, Simone, and Tiffany.

1. Redlining: The Re-Birth

Don't you dare call me red bone! That ain't a
compliment!

My complexion is not of the essence!
But only a reflection of a horror story forced without a
question, through jealousy, greed and rape
That 17% Caucasian in my blood stream makes my body
shake and blood boil because I couldn't even fathom how
my Skin was once so hated, that if I said no, it'll be
burned and hung for an audience full of white pale faces

My caramel is not to be applauded and your cocoa to be
distorted
We are all one within and I prefer to praise and bless the
equalities of our melanin

I'm not better than my sisters and brothers but rather
their keeper
My opportunities shouldn't supersede because of
"passing features"

There's no benefit to color as it's only a construct
Just soul and love, melanin and hair grease, tongue verbs
and shared beliefs

From the mother land of Pangea that keeps us all elite
Our depths are more than what the surface meets!

So don't call me red or yellow bone, there's no
celebration for that, only separation and demarcation
My ancestors still have imprints of whips on their backs
and castrations that washed bloodlines and ties that still
affect us through criminology, self hate, parent absentee
and the Chase of a euro dream that can never be reached

Can't you see, we are on the same field trip, whether
outside or in the house!
Our royalty, beauty and intelligence runs deep!
No more commemoration for the terrors that haunt us in
our sleep
No more prison to pipeline and baby mama drama in the
streets
No more coons, shucking and jiving to be a part of that
golf retreat
We need our fucking 40 acres and a mule to rebuild our
moor community!

Don't call me redbone, call me Shanikqua Renée, only a
name so unique
I was blessed to be reborn again through an ancestor
who chose for me
My advocacy was given to me and I'm never shutting up

You have no choice but to listen to me!

Don't call me redbone; see me for what I am!
What you are! What we are!
Our DNA speaks for itself, I'm no longer accepting
colorism and redlining
Just love for thyself and higher consciousness

"L'espoir renaît. Hope is reborn"
And Hope gave birth to me and named me Renée after
my god mother
Blessings pour down on me

2. Nanew

I still smell the aroma of that extra peppermint or winter
fresh gum

You chewed it near your front dentures and stuck it in
the back on your ear to save it
At night you'd wake up and chew it again
I thought that was the weirdest thing ever

But thinking of that makes me want that experience just
one more time
If only I can turn back the hands of time

Just one more time to see your beacon of light shine
through your hands
As you knead those buttermilk biscuits from scratch
With a side of instant coffee to be exact

I can still picture you sitting in the kitchen on your
wooden stool
Sweating but still graciously finger combing your gray
strands of hair to the side to protect that new hairdo

I remember those black winter boots that you wore
religiously every winter for over 20 years

I joked on them damn boots forever
Them shits looked like Santa's boots, but I miss them
dearly!
It's been 10 winters since I last seen them

It was the sparkle in your eyes when you chewed on
them pork grinds and sipped a little Moët
I can see the blue lining around your pupils enlarge as
your satisfaction heightened
I just knew I couldn't wait to grow up and take a sip of
that booze with you

It was the fearlessness of utilizing your strength to make
sure we were never dense
You walked down them stairs, pulled down your pants
and told that man, "Kiss my black ass"
That made my day; I wouldn't have had it any other
way!

It was your raspy voice on that bell Atlantic answering
machine
"Walk by faith not by sight... bye bye!" Echos in my head
at night...
212-862-4402...I'll never forget your number

Your wrinkled brown hands and curled feet
I know you were in pain but that never stopped you

from caring for me

You remember you took me on my first trip to Miami?
Everybody thought I was bugged out but I always
bragged cause Ms. Pearl was thugged out!
You dragged that walker through the sand to make sure I
was pleased

I cried the day you passed
Stuck in a trance as Kanye played on MTV
My heart skipped a beat, my soul quickly left me... I can't
breathe...
If only I can get one more day with you I swear I'll make
you happy!

I'll go to the store for you and buy your Cheetos and
Diet Pepsi
I'll take you to 125th Street to stroll around
I'll write all your recipes in a book so I won't never
forget
The photo albums and videos just don't suffice
I'd rather have you back in my life!

But I know that'll be selfish of me so I have to continue
to heal
But with my last memory of you at Lenox hill in room
711 with no heel has me ill

I don't know what you wanted to tell me that day but I
knew you were tired
I hope to see you again through the generations I acquire

3. Karmic Link

Where do I know you from?
You seem so familiar but I can't put a finger on it
But every time we speak, the fingers do link!
With this clit!
Cause every Twitter notification I get
Gets my pussy throbbing and wet

Your brown skin and chinky eyes send me to a galaxy of climaxes
Damn I think I'm ready for the D! But wait, hold on
I have to remind myself that I've only known you for 2 weeks!

But I swear you feel so familiar to me!
Like I've loved you in the past and reincarnation brought you back to me!

We finally meet on 14th street and the touch of you holding my hand is sending me!
It's so magnetic we both agreed

I got the sweats and now my wash n set ain't even set!
What the hell do I do next?
Alright now it's time to play it cool

It's the depths of your pure soul that I can see through
your eyes
It's the Burberry cologne and the way your rubbing my
thighs
As we talk about the moon and skies

It's the motivation of your speech and pronunciation of
words for me!
I think he's the one for me!
It's the chivalry you present
and purple aura that has me head over hill in fantasy
I can see it; a whole damn family!

I'm so glad that stars aligned us together
Libra and Taurus, they say we don't mix
But I don't care what's said, we in this together
Forever till eternity
I love you Dustin

4. Apartheid

Invisible lines, red lines, white lines we put in our minds
Through our nostrils, got our senses numb like Covid symptoms
and y'all know that but y'all still crewsin' the system like
Miles Latrell with the Vandergeld sisters

White supremacy, narcissism, Willie Lynch, mental slavery
All created as a way to implement a system of hate;
against ourselves...
and we still invest, let's not digress...

Whips and chains surrounding our brain waves; got us fucked up
We deadass forgot about the slave trade?!

On the ships we sailed off and became the number 1 sale
and as soon as we landed we were split, did you forget?

Our ancestors were killed, raped, chained and sold for a plant
and we're out here fighting over which flag is the best?!

African, Jamaican, Dominican, American, Haitian, Puerto

Rican, who the fuck cares
Cause in the eyes between the lines, motherfuckers only
see 1 color
and you better not cross that field line!

So what are we really fighting over?
Is it the power or the wealth?
But no matter what it is, our trauma lies so deep that
instead of fighting and comparing trivial novelties
We should be talking about our similarities because we
are all one
At least that's what I see...

Cause like Ye said "even if you in a Benz you still a nigga
in a coupe"
So let's say fuck all the lines and separation that only
cause dismay and displace
and begin a new chapter that celebrates our divinity,
royalty and DNA.

Cause we are the shit and only we know it!
So don't let those lines disintegrate our internal wealth
Let's build together and spread love cause I know damn
well our ancestors ain't want us this way
Fuck apartheid in every way!

5. Thirty.Four

3 plus 4 equals 7
You may not get it now but by the end of this poem,
You'll understand the depths of my heaven on Earth- in
literal form

Two bodies formed out of chemical love and bond
9 plus 9 equals 18 and all it took was 1 out of 8 chances
to make magic happen

The first one was 3; an inevitable dividend of the divine
Destyned to be
A true artist in a miniature form of me
Born on a holy rainy day; Yom Kippur
A true spiritual awakening and growth through
transformation and reform

But the stars weren't aligned enough
4 plus 20 equals 6 but my dear Taurean was terminated
with remiss
My heart pains every day thinking about that shit

10 plus 3 equals 4
But it wouldn't be until an entire solar year around the
sun

Which brought back that 4 that fell from my womb on
3/1
That equals 4.

But as you can see numbers don't lie and 4 fought and
strived
To be here and complete the fertilization of my family
tree
3 and 4 make Sevyn, types of fruit, so pure and sweet
Now I feel complete because my mathematics are Godly

I hope you got what I've been preaching
34 is the additions of me, of we, of us
Family

6. Codependency

I need you!
And not physically!
I need you to understand me emotionally and mentally!

I'm no longer the girl you met on Twitter in 20-10
and the woman I've become to be;
My nigga you've gotta get to know me!

I need our souls tied and actions to bring the law of
attraction
That manifests us into a universe not just another
melodrama
I don't need the theatrics; I'm thinking in the lines of
marriage

I'm tired of the soliloquies
I'm in need of a colloquy!

It's like we operate on two different stratospheres!
I don't know whether to take the red or green pill!

You frustrate me with all your fairytales and lies
For you don't understand the depth of me because of the
trauma you pry!

I'm not a door mat and will be heard!
I don't give a fuck about why you cheated with her, her,
her and HER!
My words should be heard!

I want you to hear that I love and adore you but I'm
hurting inside
You trigger daddy issues that I no longer can deny.

My insecurities start barking when I see you
But co-dependency is what I rely; On with you...

Ughh just show me you love me cause the words are no
longer coming through

I need you, to understand me
Not the girl on Twitter
But the woman I've become to be

And in order to do that I need to understand you too
Please open up for us two

7. Dear Mom: A Letter Written at the 18th Year

As you know, it's almost time for my departure
This whole month has been nothing but drama between
the both of us

Throughout the month we have either been letting the
problem pass us by
or let it build up and eat us alive

From the words "fuck you,"
I see you let it build up inside of you

Now in this point of time, most children will start to
neglect their parents
Because such harsh words can leave one feeling unloved

Being that I am old enough, I understand your reasoning
The thought of you losing your job has has been
stressing you out
and you can't handle the pressure you're under

This is normal
I love you with all my heart
and no matter what we go through

Just remember you are my mother and I am your
daughter
No one can tear us apart

Once again, I know the job situation is stressing you out
because everyone can tell
You are not only hurting yourself but others around you
Please mom, just take my advice and think positive
I appreciate and love you
I am here for you

I usually don't express my feelings towards you and I've
noticed that I should
As I go back to Buffalo, you will be on my mind and my
prayers go out to you
and just remember that someone else has it worse than
us
We are blessed

Now that you've read this message
You can do whatever you want with it
But just know that I appreciate and love you

Love,

Mookie

8. Blind

The system has failed us once again!

Children in bunks
Daddies locked up
Moms on drugs and welfare
No health care

Foster care, prevention, ACS, school, jail
It's all intertwined with a mission to lead the youth to
hell

Anti-racism, Diversity and Equity, political advocacy
It's all the same because WE are the gate keepers
Whether you want to believe it or not
We are the gaps between the bridges
But the foundation and skills we embody can never be
laid
As the policies inhibit concrete, so the bridge forever
separates

Psychotropic meds, evaluations, managed care
Only manage to exacerbate the pain

Research, Gov't funding, deception

Things will never change

Middle class, poverty, homelessness is all the same under
capitalism
Don't be fooled by the imaginary caste system
Our struggle has been written in stain through white
supremacy and disdain

Black on black crime, Black lives matter, gender equality
There's a hidden agenda that you'll are refusing to see

But being blind may just be a better fit
The terrors of seeing haunts and lures
Creates psychological warfare
Which ultimately leads us back to the initial cycle...

The system has failed us once again...

9. Walk N Ur Shoes

You couldn't walk a mile in my shoes
That's what they say
But with ambition and tenacity like I display
Fuck it, I'ma walk that mile anyway

I don't care about your trials and tribulations
Shit I got my own problems just like you...
I'm fucked up too!

And that's why I'ma walk the mile
No matter the trial or should I say the trail
Who cares about the word, just know I won't be derailed

Cause the shit that I go through, I gotta keep on stepping
But while I'm stepping I gotta make sure my shit is fly
And I know my credit line is on the verge
But the urge to cop that heat on a Saturday morning line
got me in a bind

It's tied to my soul and uplifts my Wednesday woes
Eradicates the stress connected to my ancestors welts
It just makes me feel good knowing that with all I have
going on
My feet and choice of shoes will create equilibrium and

prevent the blues

So I'ma walk that mile, no matter how long it takes
And I'm walking that mile with grace and taste

Walk N Ur Shoes...however you choose...

10. Virgo

It took me sometime to write this
For I get too emotional when I think about our distance
But I'm writing this because transparency is the only
solution to true spiritual clarity

It's been three years since we've sat down and talked
I often wonder if you think about me and miss my
company

My best friend and soulmate; we were conjoined like
twins
Even had life long plans with our children
But unforeseen events took our life for a twist

There's no one to blame for this but our lack of
emotional intelligence
We both wanted the best for our relationship and it hurts
me to my core
Seeing someone I've known for over 30 years walk away

I was hurt and felt abandoned
I cried for days wondering what role did I play
Just even writing about what transpired has me close to
tears

I never thought it would end this way

We used to laugh uncontrollably at the dumbest things
We shared the same interests and loved our summer
trips to Miami
Our boyfriends got on our nerves and we would talk
mad shit
and let the experiences fuel us up to be on some bullshit

Even our Earth signs made us compatible
Taurus and Virgo; such a harmonious friendship
It felt so stable but that one crack in the road shook us
up something serious

I hope one day we can talk it out
I miss you Charisma Shalayne
Forever my Virgo best friend

11. 1:11

The ancestors keep talking to me
But I don't know exactly what they want
or what they're trying to show me

I'm trying to find me
But I keep finding myself in the same vicious cycles of
the land of make believe

Same spirits with different faces
Same lessons in different places
Same rotation on the celestial axis; I can't catch a break
so I keep asking

But the ancestors won't talk
They just keep sending numbers and I can't shake that
shit
They're everywhere in my presence

I see it but I don't know what it means
Got me feeling like Neo in the 5th dimension
And not to mention, the source of light I keep seeing
along the 3rd dimension seems dim
Red or blue pill, fuck it I'm taking purple to see the
outcome of both

Or maybe that's why I keep ending up at the end of the
stick on the same totem pole

I feel lost and confused
Someone or something's following me and it feels sirene
1:11,11:11, 10:17, 333, 444
Numbers all around me

I can no longer ignore it
For the callings are so loud that I begin to hear whispers
in the wind
But the decoding is so faint that I begin to doubt my
internal gifts

I need clarification
I want change so bad
My faith is of a mustard seed
I'm looking for you in a dream
To tell me what's to come for the future near me

I'm going to keep listening and take heed
I think the message is going to be big
And I must follow suit to fulfill my needs

12. Chosen One

I've come to the realization that you're the chosen one
Too bright and enlightened
You shined and magnified before you arrived

You were hand chosen by Godly forces
and I am glad you picked me as a spiritual tour guide

I thought I lost you three times
But you oriented back to our consciousness
For the sake of our family ties

I've seen too many fallen ones and not too many
rainbows
But you rose out of the ashes like the Phoenix you are
To make sure there were only four leaf clovers after the
storms

You were manifested years beyond my time
A true form of perfection
A number 10; the only 1 on top
Completion and new beginnings

Three weeks early
Your arrival through the birth canal was powerful and

intense

Your smile melted my heart

and eased the pains from how you tore my vulva within

Holding you for the first time gave me a new sense of
direction

I knew from the moment I laid eyes on you, you were
our additional blessing

7/24/24, a firecracker of liberty, the ruby red cancer

The chosen one

Phoenix

13. Leyes

You ever stared at someone in their eyes
and knew they were lying?!

Let me say that again!

You ever stared at someone in their eyes
and knew they were lying?!

It was the glare in their eyes that told the truth
But while they glistened gold fairy dust,
the perception and deception in the optical view is what
you wanted to believe was true

I mean, it's all there!
The Kodak view blurred a few times
But my nigga that's your fault; you're in control of the
viewpoint
You wanted that world to be fuzzy and your gift to be
tongue tied
To the minds of those on the outside

It was all a fib times 10
Sharper than your peripheral
You wasn't able to see the wide angle lens

Now you cockeyed cause them leyes got you double tied
Bifocals can't even help
Them Medicaid lines in your lenses only clarified the
foresight and not the hindsight
So either way the vision is still blurry
or so that's what you think

You told me eye was your number 1
I couldn't have believed that was true
An eye for and eye, a toot for a toot
My BV is telling me the truth

And I'm still believing the camera view knowing damn
well after 11 pm
The question is "do you know where your children are?
Yeah I do, right in plain sight for another bitch's view

I see it in my camera on night vision as I look through a
glass house
But I won't throw stones for the potential eye only likes
the leyes

It's a sense of protection with the ability to change and
shift the reality on the holder's view
It's an escape from the truth
It allows for delusions to become more than the logical

I defend it, I own it as if it were a part of me
A plague, a disease, cancerous, it continues to grow so
deep

Somebody turn the flash on
I'm trying to see if it's just me
or will it only intensify and perfect the leyes on the
screen

Another deflection of desired perfection... leyes

14. Melanin

Melanin
Not many know what it is or how powerful it can be

Melanin
All they know is the multifaceted complexion they see
when it shines and reflects amongst the peek

Melanin
It's the only ingredient that sets us apart from the weak

Melanin
The very pigmentation that plays a specialized role in
our Afrikan features

Melanin
The pineal gland's favorite cousin
You know, the one that's always there to provide you
with the family's deepest secrets
The secrets that set us free and provide us with
spirituality
It's the secrets that no one else can duplicate or decode

Melanin
The very superpowers that are embedded in us from

birth

Don't let them tell you you're not of worth

Melanin

It's a gift only shared within the elite circles

So don't ever let a square influence your purpose

Melanin...

Dedicated to all of my brothers and sisters!

15. Literary Content: Random Thoughts at the 11th Hour

Too many of us to ever feel inferior
DNA peculiar
Melanin superior

My brown is too tough
Call me money Mayweather
I fight the hate just like Hampton during the Black
Panther Revolutionaries
It won't be televised
But the seeds will be planted; sowing and germination

Brown skin superpowers activated
Them people hella hating
I got the juice like Pac, Tobe and Fats
I represent the red, green and black across every nation
Don't matter the pattern or coordination

I speak for everyone when I say I love being black
The most hated, elevated, educated, graduated, imitated
but never celebrated

Hustle hard like T.I.
Knowledge on Raekwon
5 percent cognition
Peace to the nation

Be proud of who you are because nobody else will
Raise your fist in the air like Smith and Carlos
To show your courage and strength in your skin

Use your words not your actions
Cause that's what they're expecting
Keep your head up high
Let your black and beautiful thrive

16. Healing with You

Vulnerability has led me to this literary piece
To communicate my need for peace; with you
Because our pieces of DNA have now elevated into buds
that bloomed

Both broken and co-dependent
Our forces only force us to rely and reply to pain that
was once linked to our childhood abrasions
It cuts deep and hinders our ability to change
Jaded in our emotions but green enough to turn the
other cheek
and smile for the children's sake

But I no longer want to be fake and own up to our
mistakes
I'm ready for growth and productivity
and open to sharing my sensitivities without projecting
my deepest insecurities
You're forever my best friend before anything
This is a formal invitation to create space for emotional
rehabilitation
because I'm tired of our relationship debilitating

If you're open, I'm open too

I miss the very touch of you
I miss our echoes of laughter and intellectual debates
I want that old thing back and I also need you to crack
this back

I am hopeful for our future and what God has in store for
us
I want us to vow to individual introspection and
expressing affection
Forgiving past hurts and making conscious efforts
Balance and empathy to open a new level of intimacy
I'm ready for love once again

If you're also ready;
Take my hand and promise to reflect and repair
I believe in us and others do to
Now give me a kiss!

Love,

Your Coo Coo

17. Motherhood

Early mornings, day smiles, night cries
Postpartum depression attached to your psyche like a
leech
Sucking your life dry

Happy faces; tantrums on the floor
Attitudes across the rooms
Misunderstandings; yelling and screaming so they can
hear you

Leaking tender breast, weight gain, PCOS
Teeth gone, hearing and hair loss
Insecurities got the best of you
But the husband and children only expect the best from
you

Skin pale, facial hair, cookah dry
Out of alignment with society's beauty standards
But put a smile on my face for the betterment of my
children's mental wellness

Vertigo, edema, libido, guilt and shame
The chemical imbalances will never have me the same
I wonder if my family will accept my change

or if I'm still beautiful in the eyes of the beholder
While my girdle helps me hold up

Constant fear, dreams of perfection, never ending questions
No handbook or directions
Exploration into soft parenting
Thoughts of purchasing a belt because they keep testing

Loss of friends and companionship
Feelings of abandonment throughout parenting
The only socialization I have is with Ms. Rachel Griffin

Appreciation, soul searching isolation
Daily blessings, I might complain
But motherhood has shown me a type of love I could never explain

Empathy, new developments, paradigm shifts
New circle built on shared paths and experiences
Found family and created my own lineage

The heirs rebuild my self-esteem
Which gives me the strength to reclaim our legacy

I'm so proud to be a mother
Even though I often feel defeated and depleted

I want to thank my mother and commend her for all she
has done for me
I honestly don't know how she raised me in such scarcity

To all the mothers' out there; you got this!
No matter the triumphs you feel
Your babies bring vibrant light to your life

Forever longevity in motherhood...

18. Words of Wisdom

One

Be patient with yourself and have grace

For there are no failures in life

Experiences are our studying techniques

and our gifts are our dissertations

Two

It's okay to cry

Don't be concerned about what others say

Your tears are a sign of strength and resiliency

Three

Your reactions to trauma is your body's level of over

protection

Cheer for yourself

Maladaptive will never be accepted

Four

Be careful of the words you speak

Whether negative or positive

Your spells manifest in reality

Five

Your greatest gift is your consciousness

Remain silent and think before you speak
Let your senses analyze the stimuli and
Body be at a pure state of being

Six

Be humble and afford yourself an opportunity
To enjoy the blessings from your achievements
and spiritual deference

Seven

Heal your wounds through isolation and self-reflection
As band-aid fixes are ineffective

Eight

The person you see in the mirror is the only person
That can re-direct your insecurities
Be proud of you and let the shadows fall behind
While the sunrises

Nine

Remove items from your bag and keep it light
For your shoulders internal sign displays delicacy

Ten

Stay grounded and water your roots
Your souls will blossom and fruits will flourish

Eleven

Sawubona

See people for who *THEY* are

and they'll see *YOU* for who you are times three

19. Time

Time is not of the essence
Time is an illusion that has been created
For the masses and distresses

Time is not all we have
For the construct is only a prison to the mind
and keeps everyone in line

No matter how we slice it
The past, present and future will
Continue to play out how it was meant to be
It's the fundamental aspect of reality

Time has no restrictions
Only bureaucracies that create boundaries
For financial securities

Time is what you make of it
Don't waste it
Manage your actions without rush
Money; don't chase it

Anything you need you will be blessed with
Have faith in your next steps and make your

Next steps your best steps

Put your watch down and observe the sun
The shades of dusk till dawn will be your compass
The magnetic field will attract your deepest desires

Time
Time
Time
Is not on your side
Manage your actions with no rush

20. The Vertex Connection

Every once in awhile; we meet up again
There's a new face but it's always a better version
When I look into your eyes, I see the light
There's a plain view of purity and innocence in sight
I know that you have not been sent to harm but to
flourish the season
But at times I don't want to engage because I know
seasons end
Another friend I may lose is what I fear or regret

But I can't stay away because your aura is so clear
You bring the best out of me unintentionally
My laugh is loud when you're next to me
My thoughts are clear and goals are met expeditiously
The courage you give to me is something I purposely
reciprocate
Because it's a feeling I never want to cease once the
season ends

The tricky part is I don't know how long this season will
be
But it seems like every time we meet the seasons become
longer
and the smiles become brighter

I'm grateful for that and cherish your every moment
This is not a romance but a true friend; a twin flame or
soul mate

Our time together feels like eternity and our life paths
are carbon copies
The synchronistic timing is always fated and defining
We can't escape knowing each other, even though it may
not last very long
But the impact is powerful and meaningful; I never want
this to end

The end does come
But I realized that the person I know doesn't have to
conclude
In order for this connection to endure
I have to communicate and put my pride aside
I can't be the person hiding in isolation after missing
God's sent lesson

This is for you all
The ones who changed my life throughout the years
Even though y'all all have different faces, trust me
The links are all the same
To all my Aquarius, Gemini, Libra, Virgo, Taurus, Aries,
Cancer and Sagittarius
Thank you for exchanging love with me

Thank you for being my true friend and allowing me to
do the same
Our connections will last forever
So when you see me don't be a stranger,
or our love was a master piece

I love you all!

21. The North Node: The Realignment

To understand the assignment it took years of searching
Characteristics of an Aries in the North Node
True destination is the journey of self reclaiming
Labeled as an independent warrior but struggled to
Find harmony with the frequency of my Libra
personality
Hiding behind the fearless
I often feared what others would think of me

Not knowing who I was for so many years
Because the expectations were placed on me by parents
who were surviving aimlessly
Everyone else's goal for me was to break the cycle of
poverty
Not taking into account that such a task also includes
breaking the chains of mental slavery

My thought process is different
Some can't comprehend my actions and words
Only argue because they believe my opposition is out of
position
With the position they placed on me at birth

I was sent here to shake shit up
Not to sit around and be complacent with society's
displacement
I no longer want to take care of *WE* but to focus on *ME*

My new challenge is my soul elevation
Melancholic eliminated
No more cordial conversations and mastering the art of
keeping conflict at bay
My mission is to embrace truly what my heart desires

My creativeness will no longer be suppressed
Criticism will no longer be addressed
Impressions of the North Node will leave them pressed

Those who believe will applaud
Because they've seen me at my lowest
It's my time to shine for the sake of *ME*
I'm only fascinated with spiritual wealth and prosperity
The realignment

2+1=3